George the Giraffe
by S. Jaydee

To Sally's Grandchildren

With best wishes

From

Shirley (S. Jaydee)

LOVINGLY DEDICATED TO MY
Three grandsons who have given me many helpful
ideas for GEORGE THE GIRAFFE rhymes
and long may they continue to do so.

Many thanks to my youngest for his front cover
illustration and sincere thanks also to
Becky Howard (www.rkhoward.com) for her colourful
interpretation of all my GEORGE THE GIRAFFE
Rhymes

Last but not least, I would like to thank Sarah -
(www.amazon.com/Sarah-Bevan-Fischer) for her
invaluable help.

Musings from "Maesgwyn" have led me to write about

GEORGE THE GIRAFFE

As I recovered from Cancer

My spirits were lifted as I soon discovered
It did help, by making me smile
As several years later I feel I've recovered
Much more than I did for a while

This animal helped in my Cancer recovery
For I'm living proof, all the time
By describing light humour, was a discovery
So now I write nonsense in rhyme

My verses were formed right out of the blue
For an animal sounding forlorn
I chose a Giraffe who lived in a Zoo
That's exactly how Georgie was born.

Contents

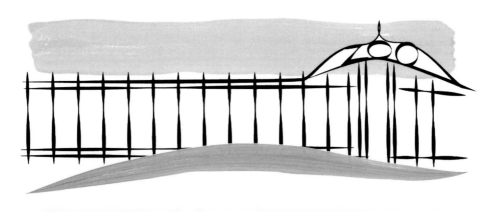

A LOVESICK GIRAFFE

She brought me my dinner dressed up as a maid
And promised to come back again
I'm terribly lonely and get so afraid
Too shy, I should have asked 'when'?

But now every Thursday she comes to see me
Arriving exactly at noon
She's a very sweet lady and tells me they're free
Thursdays don't come round too soon

I'm terribly cold stuck here in the Zoo
And no one to talk to ---- just her
I look forward to visits, I'm sure you would too
But I shiver in spite of my fur

There's snow all around, it covers the ground
And I have to venture out there
This might sound so silly, but I think I've found
Someone for whom I could care

She took pity on me and made me a scarf
A lovely bright stripy one too
It took her a while, and I had to laugh
Getting it on was quite a to do!

When all said and done, I'm used to the heat
My birthplace I frequently mourn
We didn't have snow, and neither had sleet
In Africa where I was born

I think I may have made a good friend
As I'm warmer now, thanks to her scarf
I'm flattered by her, but I know it's pretend
For I'm a four legged long necked Giraffe !!!

1

GEORGIE'S ADVENTURES

Have you ever seen Georgie riding a bike
Well neither had I until now
It had been a dream but you know what it's like
The unanswered question was how?

You see, he has forelegs as well as the hind
So the puzzle was how he would cope
Being so determined with nerves left behind
The others all thought it a joke

He eventually perched on top of the seat
Though initially wobbled as well
But he wouldn't give in and gave us a grin
So he lost concentration and fell

What is quite surprising, is all he's accomplished
On days when he helps at the Zoo
In fact his talents have certainly flourished
Depending on your point of view

His next adventure's going to be grand
As he's anxiously wanting to drive
The rules of the road, he must understand
As they're there to help him survive

Encouraging him to do a good deed
They allowed him to work in the Zoo
So when the animals came round to feed
They were glad he was someone they knew

He wanted a car but that was bazaar
As that might have started a trend
Which surely would cause a massive hoo-ha
And who knows just where it could end

So a tractor was bought and Georgie was taught
But everyone started to laugh
Delivering their food, who would have thought
Was a four legged long necked giraffe!!!

THE CHOIR

Now Georgie's adventures started off well
He wanted to please the Zoo Keeper
He'd recovered from bruises the day that he fell
Then decided to keep the Zoo cleaner

So he found a large bucket, a brush and a mop
And proceeded to sweep out a cage
But he upset the lion who told him to stop
As he warned, he'd get in a rage

George knew he was moody, now more than ever
So went in the monkey's enclosure
In such awful weather they huddled together
Not wanting to die from exposure

Then suddenly George had a brainstorm
He found them some woollies to wear
In order to keep the animals warm
Except those with plenty of hair

He put up a notice for all to enquire
Those wanting to try something new
Would anyone like to sing in a choir?
All at once they were forming a queue

The frogs gave a croak for a bit of a joke
But the monkeys gave squeals of delight
Then it went quiet and nobody spoke
Seeing the lion, they scattered in fright

But soon they regained a relative calm
As the lion took up his position
Now reassured they'd come to no harm
He gave them a roaring rendition.

3

BIRTHDAY PARTY

Georgie was good at arranging events
And he knew Zebra's Birthday was near
Nobody else had a clue what to do
So he was the one volunteer

He had to devise a Party surprise
While others were kept in the dark
To get too excited would be so unwise
Especially the squealing Aardvark

He booked a Magician, who lived fairly near
Which added to all the confusion
As some of them feared they'd soon disappear
But he told them 'It's just an illusion'

The planned secret Party was well advertised
As somebody found the balloons
The secret was out, so Georgie advised
Ignoring the guilty Baboons

Balloons were hanging from bars of their cage
They were there for all to see
Being so excited, because of their age
But now banned from the Birthday Tea

A parcel was passed and thrown in the air
And landed in Kangaroo's pouch
The Hyena laughed as he couldn't care
He said he heard Kanga cry 'Ouch'!

He then suggested an egg and spoon race
Before they started to feed
But it rapidly turned into such a disgrace
As it started a massive stampede

All hell was let loose, they liked playing that game
The keeper and all of his staff
Knew who to blame of course and his name
Poor Georgie, the long necked giraffe.

HEDGE TRIMMER

George had decided to look for some work
But he had no idea what to do
And then he was told of some work with a perk
As it could only be done by a few

He was luckily born with a very long neck
Which made him exceedingly tall
His boss was to find his work hard to check
And more often he didn't at all

George was faced with high hedges to trim
And the perk of the job was that he
Could eat any leaves that appealed to him
While creating some topiary

So George was taken to a beautiful place
Then given a thingumabob
To trim all the sides without leaving a trace
And told to get on with the job

When all said and done, he was having such fun
Whilst trying to be realistic
He was hoping his flare, when the trimming was done
Could be described as artistic

The hedges were cut, which changed the landscape
For the leaves at the top he could chew
Clever or not, he had changed their shape
Depending on your point of view

The job was quite easy and simply enjoyed
As easy as ABC
Although he'd been clever, his boss was annoyed
Sadly it turned out to be

A day for poor George that would be his last
For a crowd had gathered to laugh
At the hedges he'd cut, as people walked past
Were all shaped like long necked Giraffes!!!

A HOLIDAY

There were a few things Georgie bothered about
Things that he wanted to do
As years had gone by he'd felt he'd missed out
After all, he lived in a zoo

A holiday had only been just a dream
But now he felt he could cope
He felt it would boost his own self-esteem
To go on a train was his hope

So he went to the station like ordinary folk
But due to his height, they refused
When he asked for a seat they thought it a joke
And Georgie was just not amused

Because Georgie's neck was terribly long
A carriage was changed for a truck
He thought it unfair and said it was wrong
It was small and soon he was stuck

The train followed the line towards the Welsh coast
Going clickety clack as it went
He tried to get free, he did, well almost
But his legs and his neck were all bent

Grabbing hold of forelegs, two men gave a shout
While others pulled those at the rear
He felt so ashamed as he nearly fell out
All those on the train gave a cheer

So embarrassed he ran as fast as he could
To have fun his chances looked grim
He heard lots of shouting and then understood
The people were looking for him

There was somebody waving way out in the sea
Without any sign of a boat
He realised they were in difficulty
Perhaps he could help them to float

It was George to the rescue, George who could cope
He walked right into the sea
His head stuck out like a periscope
But he brought them ashore, to safety

His dream of a holiday turned out to be
Only two days and a half
But the news of the day, was a rescue at sea
By a hero - a long necked Giraffe!!!

HIS RETURN

George didn't feel like he'd been away
Only his friend knew he'd gone
You can't call two days a real holiday
Something was definitely wrong

This time he decided to take his good friend
Who needed a holiday too
Last time a postcard he'd promised to send
Was a deed he'd forgotten to do

So he went back again to the coastline of Wales
He remembered the sea and the sand
This time he hoped he'd return with some tales
And who knows he may get suntanned

He hoped there'd be no further mishap
Before, a boy nearly drowned
But George was determined to find a suntrap
He just didn't want to be found

To relax and forget and simply chill out
Was all he was hoping for
But after a rest and a good walkabout
He found a new Marine Store

He hoped he could buy some bright red lifebelts
In the shop called " Nautical Needs"
Last time his help was really heartfelt
His head was full of good deeds

The people weren't sure, as Georgie walked out

For right on top of his head
Were bright red round earrings, but was there
some doubt?
They felt that they'd been misled

Then George appeared grinning, from one ear
to ear
He always was full of surprises
But then he told those, who wanted to hear
It wasn't one of his disguises

Make no mistake, there were two of them there
One being Georgina Giraffe
Who he then introduced, and had to declare
His friend was a long necked Giraffe!!!

THE KITE

Some things are worse, but for now just imagine
When loud youngsters arrived on the beach
As their kite became tangled they made such a
din
They wondered if Georgie could reach

The kite had been blown high up in a tree
George offered to give them a hand
Of course it was done only figuratively
But most people do understand!

The friendliest people he found were Welsh folk
But had a distinct disadvantage
By not understanding what some people spoke
He'd soon have to learn a new language

Since staying in Wales he could tell all his
friends
His holiday had been abroad
He'd crossed a long bridge, a long way to the end
Now he did wish he'd brought his surfboard

But the following day getting ready to swim
The same noisy youngsters were there
They offered their kite, and just on a whim
He thought he'd have fun, for a dare

He ran down the beach with the kite in the air
And felt the force of the breeze
As he ran, he knocked over a chair
And became a flying trapeze

He held on for dear life, afraid to let go
But a gust sent him down on the sand
He got to his feet, so embarrassed you know
Further fun, he knew he'd be banned!

Can you picture poor Georgie high up in the air
Too young for an epitaph
I bet noisy youngster did much more than stare
At Georgie the airborne Giraffe!!!

A RESCUE

Georgina and George fully trained, on patrol
On the beach for most of the day
It did turn out to be quiet on the whole
But they'd made up their minds they would stay

She wore the red lifebelts on top of each ear
And felt they were very becoming
She thought they were earrings "Do you like
them my dear?"
But compliments weren't fast in coming!

"They're meant to save lives Georgina, my dear!
If someone's unable to swim
Lifebelts weren't designed to be worn as
headgear
They're either for her or for him"

Then all of a sudden they heard someone shout
It couldn't have come from the sea
They looked down the beach and then turned
about
There he was, on the cliff, by the tree

A boy went beyond the pools and the rocks
The fact was, he'd climbed up too high
When he looked down it came as a shock
He was frightened and thought he would die

At the base of the cliff, Georgie stood still
While the boy wrapped his arms round his neck
As he slid to the ground which the boy thought
was 'brill'
Promised next time he would check

Two people came running towards the Lifeguard
They were extremely alarmed
They'd lost sight of their son on the promenade
So thankful to find him unharmed

"Many thanks to you George, you're a splendid
Lifeguard
We must take your photograph!
Who would have thought after searching so hard
He'd be saved by a long necked Giraffe"!!!

9

FARMHAND

Ever since George said he wanted to drive
Not a car, but a tractor instead
Still being a learner, he had to contrive
A way to help someone called Ted

Ted was a farmer who worked on the land
And the Zoo Keeper had no objection
He agreed that George could be a farmhand
Who's work he described as perfection

Georgie was really a talented artist
Especially designing the crops
Whilst everything grew, there were parts that
he'd missed
He'd really pulled out all the stops

For there, right before him, the naughty Giraffe
Had crops grown in circular swathes
He'd managed as usual to make others laugh
At the end of his Crop Circle days

So anxious to help, and keep in his 'good books'
He drove the tractor all day
The newly ploughed field took on a new look
And that Summer he baled all the hay

But everything went too well at the start
Something was waiting to 'give'
When Ted saw his work, it was time to depart
Georgie was lucky to live

So furious with George, Ted gave him the sack
For what he had done in the field
He knew even then, he'd never go back
As his work so clearly revealed

The farmer felt Georgie must understand
In future to do as he's told
To stick to the job and not try to be grand
So his talent could slowly unfold

But this time he'd gone a little too far
So demonstrating his wrath
"Return to the Zoo and stay where you are"
Said Ted, to the long necked Giraffe!

SCARECROW

Georgie's head was so full of more crazy ideas
So guess what the new one would be?
The wisest thing would be a change of career
But he didn't give guarantees

So after the Crop Circle Catastrophe
He thought he'd better lie low
So he offered to help, but this time for free
And dressed up as a shabby scarecrow

Because he had frightened a few of the rooks
When ploughing the fields up before
They sought their revenge, and they undertook
A punishment using their claws

Now George had to stand really still in the field
And had promised that he would be good
So he flicked his long tail, which served as a shield
But he had to remain where he stood

I don't know if you knew but George made a noise
A weird unusual sound
The rooks annoyance made George lose his poise
He called out, and spun round and around

So as they fell off feeling giddy and sick
George breathed a sigh of relief
As the farmer appeared angry, and waved a big stick
He'd seen they were giving him grief

With his first time in trouble, I'm sure you'd agree
'Though almost too good to be true
His talent was noticed, now many could see
You have to give credit where due

His eyes then lit up as he saw a good chance
Of making a small extra income
He welcomed the public, they could tell at a glance
So famous his work had become

They cheered and they waved while up in the air
From there they had a good view
The basket held plenty in seven feet square
They agreed it was very good value

It didn't take long for a Hot Air Balloon
With a basket beneath on behalf
Of those wanting to view, but not before noon
"Crop Circles " cut by a Giraffe.

THE CIRCUS

As things were so quiet, the first time in ages
The Zoo Keeper said they could follow
The people who'd been in to Spring Clean the cages
While the Hippos just wanted to wallow

George wanted to plan a special day out
So everyone there could enjoy
A day at the Circus, that's what it's about
He hadn't been there since a boy

They all went by train this particular day
And the engine pulled a long truck
The Ring Master's face showed utter dismay
The animals then were dumbstruck

The Circus was shut, there was nothing to do
The animals were feeling unwell
It seems they'd all been struck down by 'flu'
This news was another bombshell

George had a word with those from the Zoo
And asked if they would agree
To do a few tricks, he was sure that they knew
To save a catastrophe

They got so excited, they'd do what they could
He was sure that somehow they'd cope
So the bears did some juggling right where they stood
And the monkeys did tricks on the rope

The animals did do a marvellous job
Spinning plates was the noisiest of all
Some did a trick with a thingamabob
And Humpty had a great fall

So George had a practise upon the trapeze
But he had to avoid getting tangled
He managed to swing with the greatest of ease
Then on the way back he just dangled

The safety net saved him from having a fall
So lucky the ropes didn't snap
The Orangutan suddenly played with a ball
Just briefly as a stopgap

It really was a tremendous success
Even Zebra showed off her new calf
While the audience cheered, they had to confess
It was all down to George the Giraffe!

12

THATCHING

There was an old cottage within the Zoo grounds
That badly needed a roof
The other collapsed just as bad as it sounds
No longer was it rainproof

Some of the animals could not understand
Why George was keen to go out
He had to make plans, well beforehand
When there weren't many people about

Today was the day, it was his intention
To ask all the others if they
Would keep it a secret, not even mention
That he was going out for the day

He'd put in an order for plenty of straw
And the elephant was his assistant
Who thought it was lunch, and told to ignore
George was this time insistent

With George's long neck and the elephant's trun
He knew they could easily reach
For the fiddly bits he had the chipmunk
'Though realised he would have to teach

Having prepared the roof to be thatched
Thought to be a dying art
Last time the roof had only been patched
He hoped now they'd think he was smart

But where was the chipmunk, so tiny and small
They called out but nothing was heard
They had to conclude that he had had a fall
But thought that must be absurd

There wasn't a sign of where he could be
Then all of a sudden they saw
The chipmunk had hidden inside the chimney
With a flag which he held in his paw

And George can never resist having fun
So hoped he'd give them a laugh
The chimney stuck out of the new thatch he'd done
In the shape of a long necked Giraffe.

TRAIN DRIVER

The things George had ventured to try in the past
Were fun and exciting to do
Though once or twice left people feeling aghast
And surprised the crowds that he drew

He thought he'd try something that was more sedate
Where danger wasn't included
Georgie might just be the right candidate
As no one wished him to be wounded

He offered to help at the local train station
And the Zoo Keeper had no objection
The guard waved his flag with a look of despair
As the driver had caught an infection

So George stoked the engine, the train went for miles
Through beautiful countryside
Having gone through a tunnel, it was no time to smile
As George looked undignified

Emerging from darkness, you should have been there
His face was covered with soot
He couldn't avoid it, he made people stare
I wonder what else is afoot

The Zoo Keeper made him stand under the shower
He didn't object to the water
It was down to the fact that he turned to full power
And was there for an hour and a quarter

Having experienced a day as Train Driver
He offered his autograph
He'd even considered a charge of a fiver
Not bad, for a long necked Giraffe!

HIDE AND SEEK

George always does have unusual ideas
He likes to keep everyone happy
Conveniently, there weren't any sightseers
Today, they would have to be snappy

Their aim was to hide in the Zoo Keeper's house
A real game of hide and seek
With eight of them there, as quiet as a mouse
And ordered that they mustn't peek

They took it in turns and closed both their eyes
And they counted to ninety two
They opened the drawers and found all his ties
But the wardrobe hid Kangaroo

Some of them found an unusual place
Like Monkey, who saw the teapot
In jumped the baby and Ma found no trace
It's one child she sadly forgot

While baby was hiding, it's mother decided
She'd make use of the stripy tea-cosy
The handle was quite uniquely provided
By the tail of the adult Ma Monkey

The Llama lay down behind the settee
While baboons hid under the bed
They rejoiced for a while that they were all free
Before it was time to be fed

But George found the funniest place by the door
And he certainly made them all laugh
With the shade on his head, as the lamp on the floor
Was George, the long necked Giraffe!

15

HOT AIR BALLOON

George thought of hiring a Hot Air Balloon
It could be a fantastic day out
He'd select one or two to befriend the baboon
In the hope they wouldn't fall out

He didn't want that to literally be
The outcome of his special treat
So he made up a list and then he could see
Where he might need to be more discrete

It just wouldn't pay to fight in the air
The basket might wobble a lot
Their weight and their size, especially the bear
Might have to be juggled somewhat

The day came around and places were found
For those he knew would get on
George was in charge and all were spellbound
As the Zoo disappeared, it had gone

The animals cheered and some gave a shout
As they didn't often go far
This was a day, they'd long talk about
So lucky to be where they are

Then all of a sudden they all gave a shout
It looked like they were going down
The flame lost it's power, should they bale out
In the lake, far below, might they drown?

But George was in charge and had a brainwave
He told them to take a deep breath
As they let their breath go, he knew it would save
All of them from certain death

The balloon then rose up in a cloudless sky
Re-inflated with animal's air
Maybe one of those times we shouldn't ask why
Someone other than Georgie took care

They all landed safely with a bit of a bump
And they did have a really good laugh
Although Bear gave a growl, being a bit of a grump
And blamed George the long necked Giraffe!!!

BIPLANE

An Air Display notice was shown in the town
And George really wanted to go
He asked for permission and put his name down
To miss it would be a real blow

They were flying a Lancaster and a Biplane
And the latter appealed to our George
He'd love to go up, but some thought insane
But an interest, you just have to forge

They wondered if he was at all acrobatic
For sometimes on a Biplane
You'd see people walking, he'd be ecstatic
But he thought some would surely complain

This time he thought he'd be more laidback
And enjoy the fresh air on his face
He didn't want that to be a drawback
Or stall and be a disgrace

But just to sit there and experience the thrill
Of flying a craft through the air
As long as the Lancaster showed off it's skill
By missing him, he didn't care

That one's a lot faster and noisier too
And not very many exist
So he took advantage enjoying the view
It was something he couldn't resist

But they understood Georgie, feeling as he
Having always admired Pilot's skill
Was a chance that he took, and most would
agree
The risk is there, always to thrill

While Georgie's excitement affects even those
Like Georgina who wore a headscarf
In fact the whole crowd clapped as they rose
To praise George, the long necked Giraffe !!!

PUTTING AND GOLF

George had held Parties and Choirs in the Zoo
And done all manner of things
So to organise Fun, was not hard to do
As everyone liked Surprise Outings

So he took them to practise at Putting to see
If they did have an eye for the ball
There was a coach there but he wanted a fee
So they learned by themselves, if at all!

As it turned out, they weren't at all bad
So the next step was the Golf Course
They realised George was a bit of a lad
But some rules he had to enforce

They were not allowed to pick up the balls
Nor could they sit down and rest
Misbehaviour would surely be their downfall
These were orders and not a request

With Georgie's forelegs spread really wide
He held the club in his teeth
The ball hit a tree though his skill he'd applied
Which unfortunately fell underneath

Now George had got a difficult challenge
Being far away from the green
The animals watched and dared him to whinge
As he was the one who'd been keen

As no one was looking, those naughty Meerkats
Picked up all the balls and they ran
When George caught them up, all they gave was
backchat
Then they hid behind Pelican

George now had a clue where the balls might be
hidden
His pouch had been useful before
In future the Meerkats would all be forbidden
And would forfeit their tea furthermore

Excluding the Meerkats, to round off the day
George thought they might like to play Bingo
Now clear of the fairway, they shouted Hooray!
The winner was Florence Flamingo

Winning some money was so unexpected
So Florence decided that half
Could now go towards whatever's collected
By George the long necked Giraffe!!!

Teaching

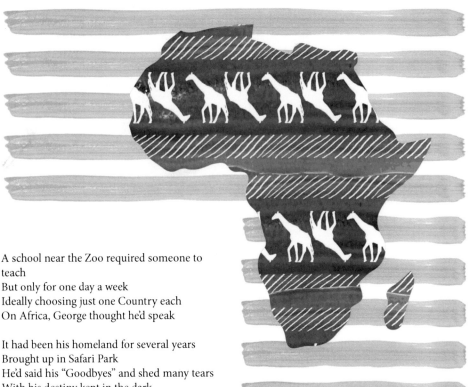

A school near the Zoo required someone to
teach
But only for one day a week
Ideally choosing just one Country each
On Africa, George thought he'd speak

It had been his homeland for several years
Brought up in Safari Park
He'd said his "Goodbyes" and shed many tears
With his destiny kept in the dark

But he did settle down in the Zoo near the town
And he hoped that he wouldn't miss them
He agreed that he would return by sundown
While enjoying a sample of freedom

But it wasn't the same, he did miss being home
So the best thing he thought he could do
Was to show the schoolchildren, where he used
to roam
In the hope that he'd interest a few

Upon the blackboard he drew a huge map
And said Rangers are needed because
Of the harm poachers do when they use a trap
And pointed to where the Park was

When George had been caught, they had used
a dart
A perfectly harmless treatment
Then it was time for his new life to start
His job being a happy agreement

He enjoyed the new challenge of teaching those
To write a brand new paragraph
Now they'd been taught with some lines in prose
By a four legged long necked Giraffe!!!

TRAVEL

One day when George returned to the Zoo
He stopped near the Zoo Keeper's house
There on the TV they showed Dr. Who
Quite enough to frighten a mouse

As George had an excellent imagination
And travel had long been a dream
Going back in time to a destination
Was possibly rather extreme

The more he thought of it, he felt that he
With pictures and stories as well
Could encourage the animals convincingly
To believe it all, who can tell?

So after giving it much careful thought
He hired a large Theatre Hall
There on the screen, just like they'd been taught
Was the scene of the Great Chinese Wall

The next thing they knew, they'd fallen asleep
But felt sure they were where they'd been shown
Hypnosis had worked, in a trance, that was deep
They were there, relaxed, they were prone

China was where lots of soldiers were found
Consisting of brown Terra Cotta
Hundreds were buried deep under the ground
To view them, you're a Globetrotter

They were lucky when passing bamboo by the
road
That Panda was back in the Zoo
He might be confused, was this his abode?
Just as well he didn't go too

When they were woken and questioned if they
Had just been transported through space
George wondered if he could actually say
The truth, or would he lose face

Being honest, George just had to admit
He'd used some Tomfoolery
But the hypnosis bit he thought he'd omit
And blamed it on poor memory

They couldn't imagine where they'd go next
All wanting a new photograph
The one on the Wall was on the pretext
Of smiling at George the Giraffe!!!

An Island Escape

A very small island off the Welsh coast
Called Sully, where George liked to stay
The animals knew it was where he liked most
But aware of the dangerous tideway

So George persuaded his pals from the Zoo
To listen to important instructions
They crossed the Causeway without any issue
Knowing there'd only be ructions

Disregarding advice has left many stranded
When staying at the seaside
Some causing trouble as soon as they landed
Surrounded by swirling riptide

Kangaroo's tail just got in the way
And Meerkats ran after their brother
But all said and done, they played in the spray
Then decided to chase one another

They forgot the riptide while having such fun
As swirling water came near
"It was time" George said, "Come here everyone
Before you all disappear"

The little ones climbed onto his back
And slowly crept up his long neck
George hadn't got far when he had to backtrack
The animals first he must check

Just as well that he did, for monkeys were
missing
Which made Georgie really annoyed
He called out their names and found they were
fishing
They thought he'd become paranoid

They'd really been lucky with both fish and crabs
They didn't want to leave yet
They'd developed a system of dives and grabs
And thoroughly enjoyed getting wet

But the animal who'd caught much more than
most
With a bill and a pouch, well! You can!
The penguins were next, but pipped at the post
As the winner was Pelican

It was time to get off the Island in Wales
Before they alarmed the Zoo Staff
To make it much safer they walked holding tails
Instructed by George the Giraffe!!!

PRIDE AND COURTSHIP

George can't believe the pride that he felt
When a baby was given his name
As this very special baby's been dealt
A fortune, a title and fame

For wee baby George is already a Prince
And William will one day be King
Being married to Katherine they'll help to convince
The importance of good parenting

Now George the Giraffe has had an idea
That maybe it's time that he wed
And quite by chance he did overhear
That Georgina thought him well-bred

So George and Georgina began their courtship
And made them all smile at the Zoo
The animals laughed and started to gossip
Now starting quite a to-do

He dressed as a Waiter, she as a Maid
Remembering the lady who had
Been to the Zoo and the scarf she had made
When he was merely a lad

The meal that she'd made and the standard she set
Made him realise what to look for
Georgina now cared and was glad that they'd met
"Please marry me on the seashore"?

There could only be one animal there
To think of a bright coloured scarf
Maybe next time she'll knit them a pair
As there'll be two long necked Giraffes!!!

GEORGIE'S EARLY ADVENTURES

Now that the Royal Baby's been born
It's natural to watch his progress
George dreams of the day that he will be drawn
To the Zoo, he has to confess

He knows he'll be told of the animals there
But sadly it won't be this year
In time he'll discover some are quite rare
Before they do disappear

Will he be told of the things Georgie's done?
He's been quite a naughty Giraffe
His antics have ranged from tractors for fun
To driving a train, for a laugh

He helped with some cleaning, but upset the
Lion
While thinking of something quite new
To encourage the animals, he used a mid-iron
While golfing away from the Zoo

The Birthday Party that Georgie arranged
Just led to a manic kerfuffle
Of eggs and spoons, cross words were exchanged
So Party Plans need a reshuffle

As for the hedges that he tried to shape
Like himself, it was rather cheeky
You could say from boredom he tried to escape
But to see them was really quite freaky

Redeeming himself, he did save a boy
By wading out into the sea
The Hero returned next time to enjoy
Time with his wife, (soon to be)

He played with a kite, becoming airborne
And saved a boy from a cliff
Being sacked from the farm, left him so forlorn
As George was full of mischief

As for Crop Circles, he knew that was wrong
And then he charged for the view
From the Hot Air Balloon, some went along
To see if the rumour was true

From Circus, Thatching and playing Hide and
Seek
To blowing up all kinds of balloon
His techniques have been somewhat unique
There's never a quiet afternoon

Now flying and teaching, to mention two more
Are interests to share on behalf
Of Zoo animals, who are happy I'm sure
Thanks to George, the long necked Giraffe !!!

GEORGIE'S MARRIAGE

George and Georgina decided to wed
In the Spring of the following year
The keeper suggested their Banns should be read
As their love was abundantly clear

So a date for their Wedding was set in the Spring
And they hoped that the day would be fine
Then George had to save for a suitable ring
With a most unusual design

To bring special memories of their Homeland
He thought Georgina could wear
An outline of Africa on a wide band
Of gold, to wear in her hair

They enjoyed all the planning and some secrecy
While everyone wanted to know
They couldn't ask much out of polite courtesy
The question was, could they all go?

Africa was, somewhere special to stay
For a luxury honeymoon treat
Georgie knew it was a very long way
To bask in the African heat

While under the stars they both realised
There was much to look forward to
'Though now in their birthplace, they still both decide
Their home was back in the Zoo

So then the Zoo Keeper had to inform
Every member of staff
That Georgie now had a wife to keep warm
And would care for Georgina Giraffe!!!